VOCABIRDS

VOCABULARY WORKBOOK

GRADE 4

An imprint of Om Books International

Silence Please!

Spot the words with silent letters and draw a star below them.

Voca tip: Silent letters are not pronounced in a word.

Why So Silent?

Help the Vocabird spot and circle the silent letters in the words below.

Silent Maze

Help the Vocabird reach its food by following the path that has words with silent letters.

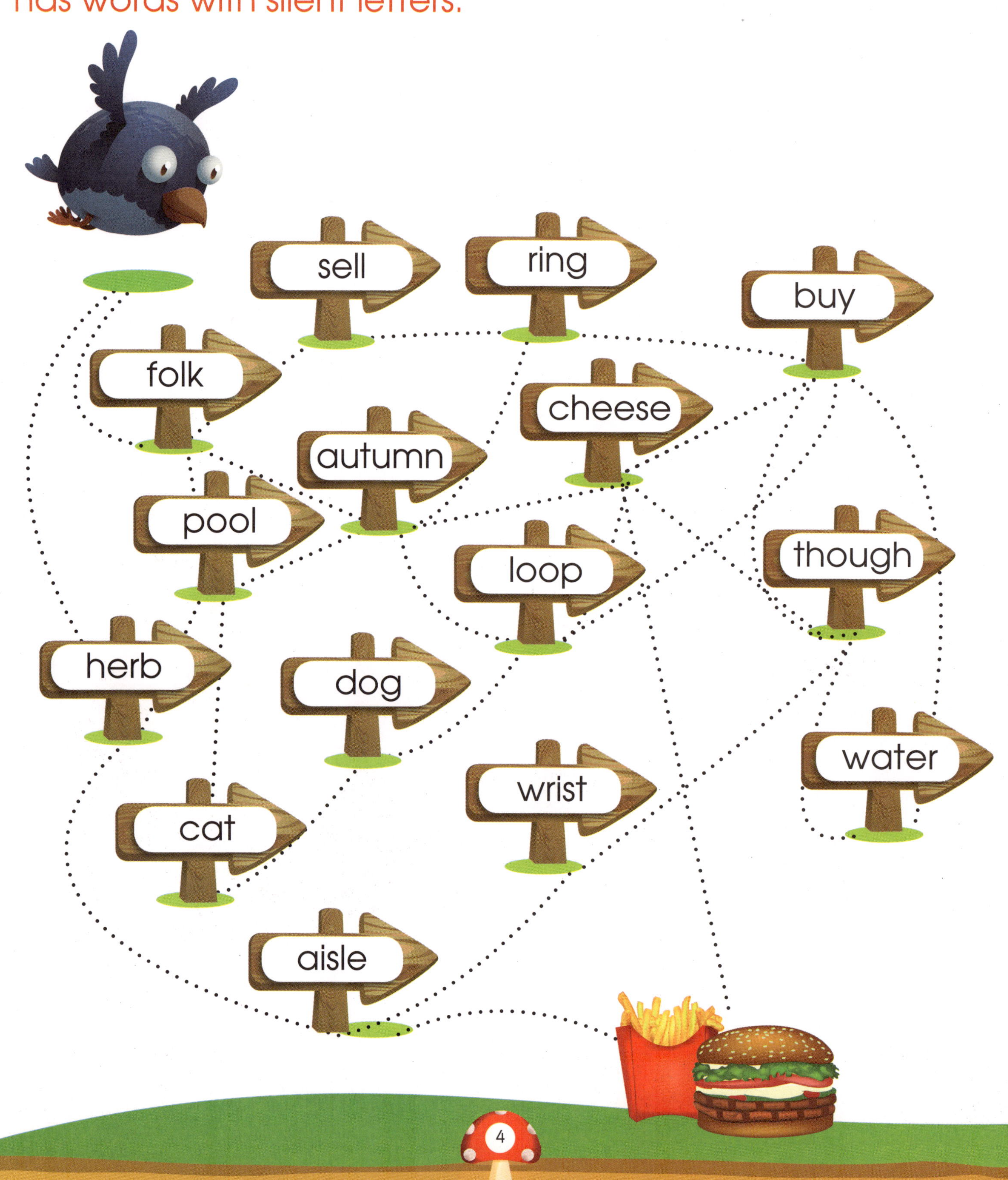

Syllable World

Help the Vocabird count the number of syllables in each word and write the number on the blanks below.

Voca tip: A syllable is a unit of pronunciation with a vowel in it. For e.g., the word "cake" has one syllable, but "paper" has two syllables – "pa" and "per".

Fishing For Syllables

Help the Vocabird read the words on each fish and break them into syllables on the plates below.

Gender Bender

Match these animals to their male and female names in the boxes.

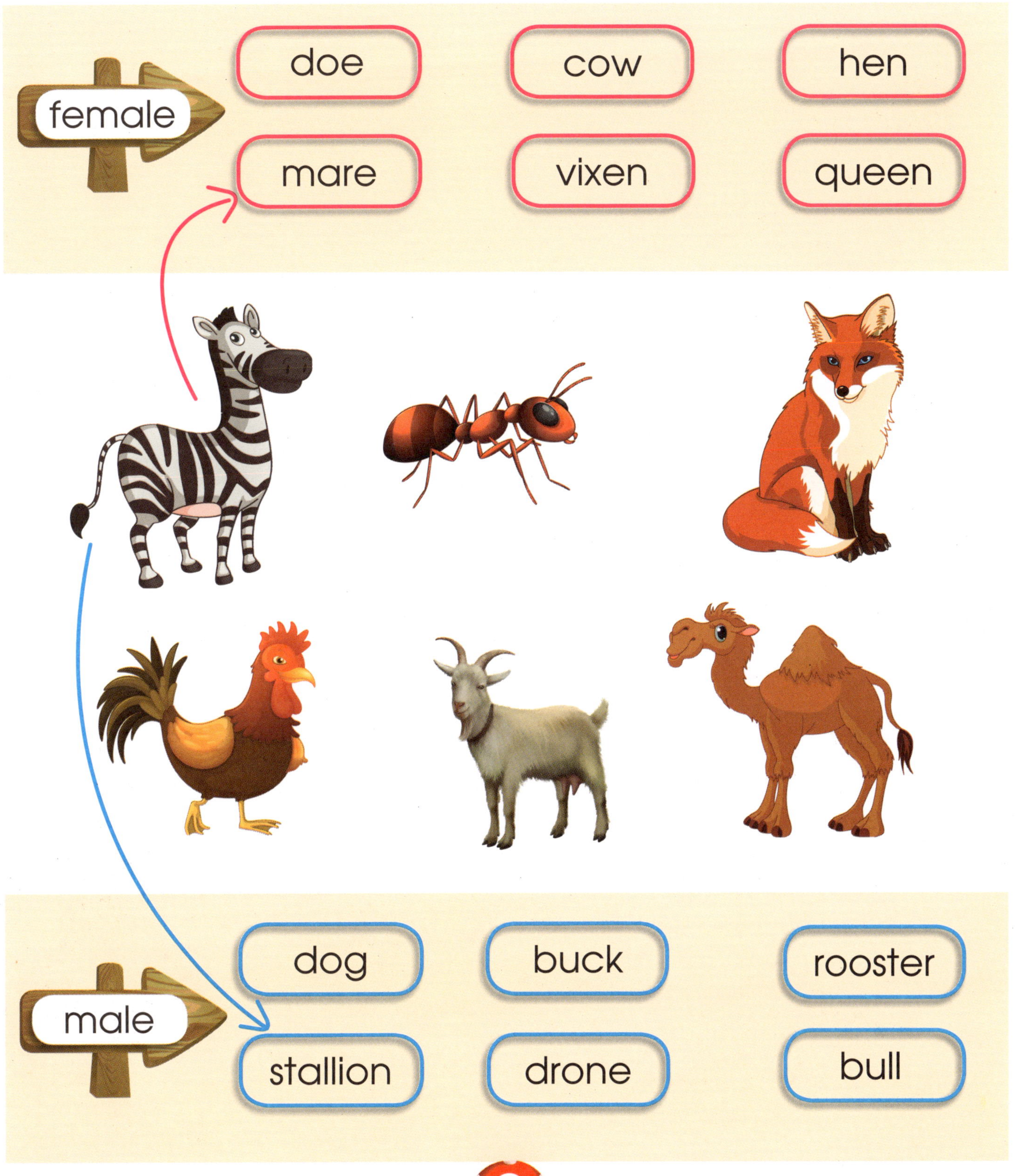

Lost Habitats

Help the Vocabird match the animals names to their habitats.

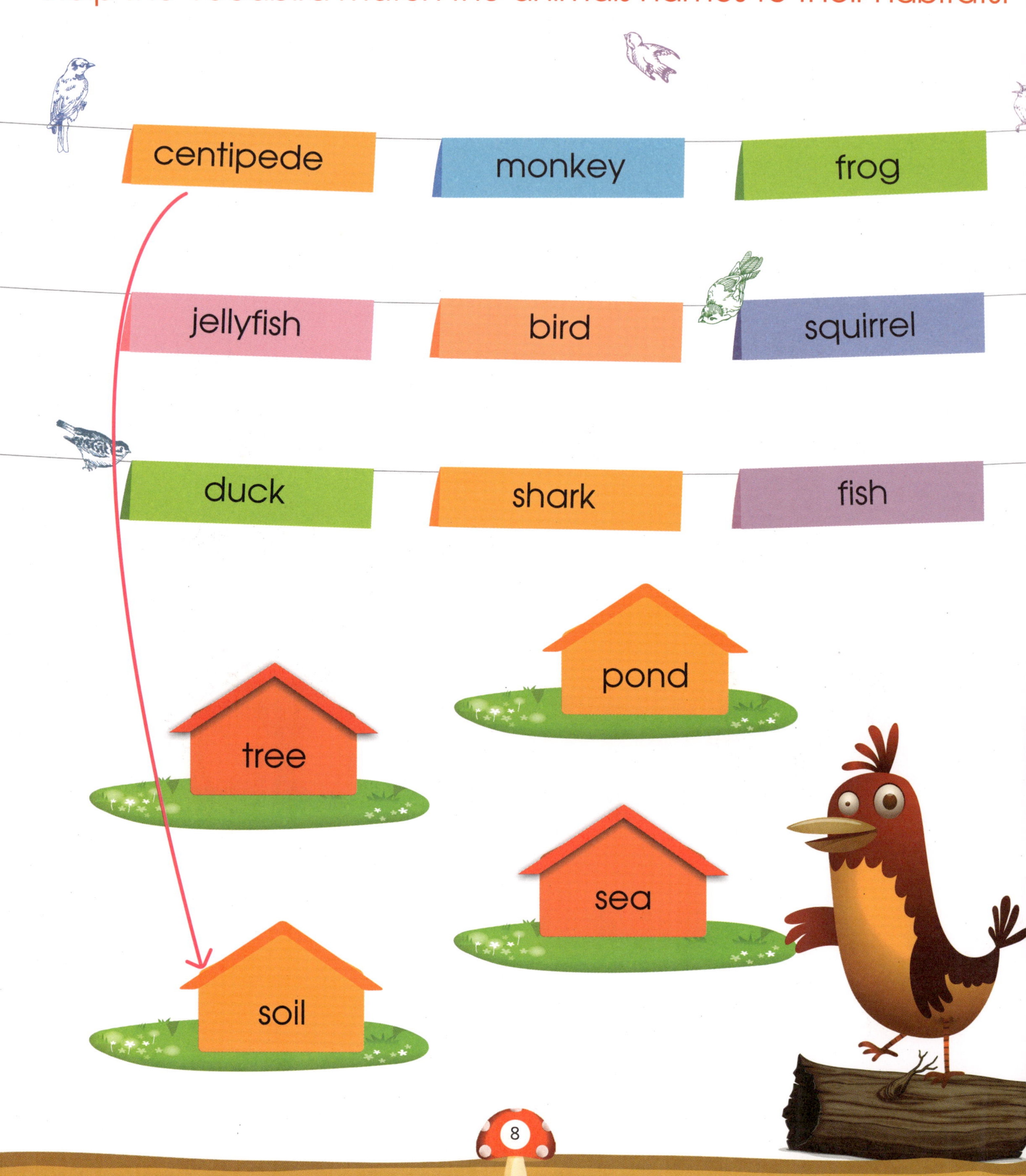

Junior Match

Match the baby animals to their correct names.

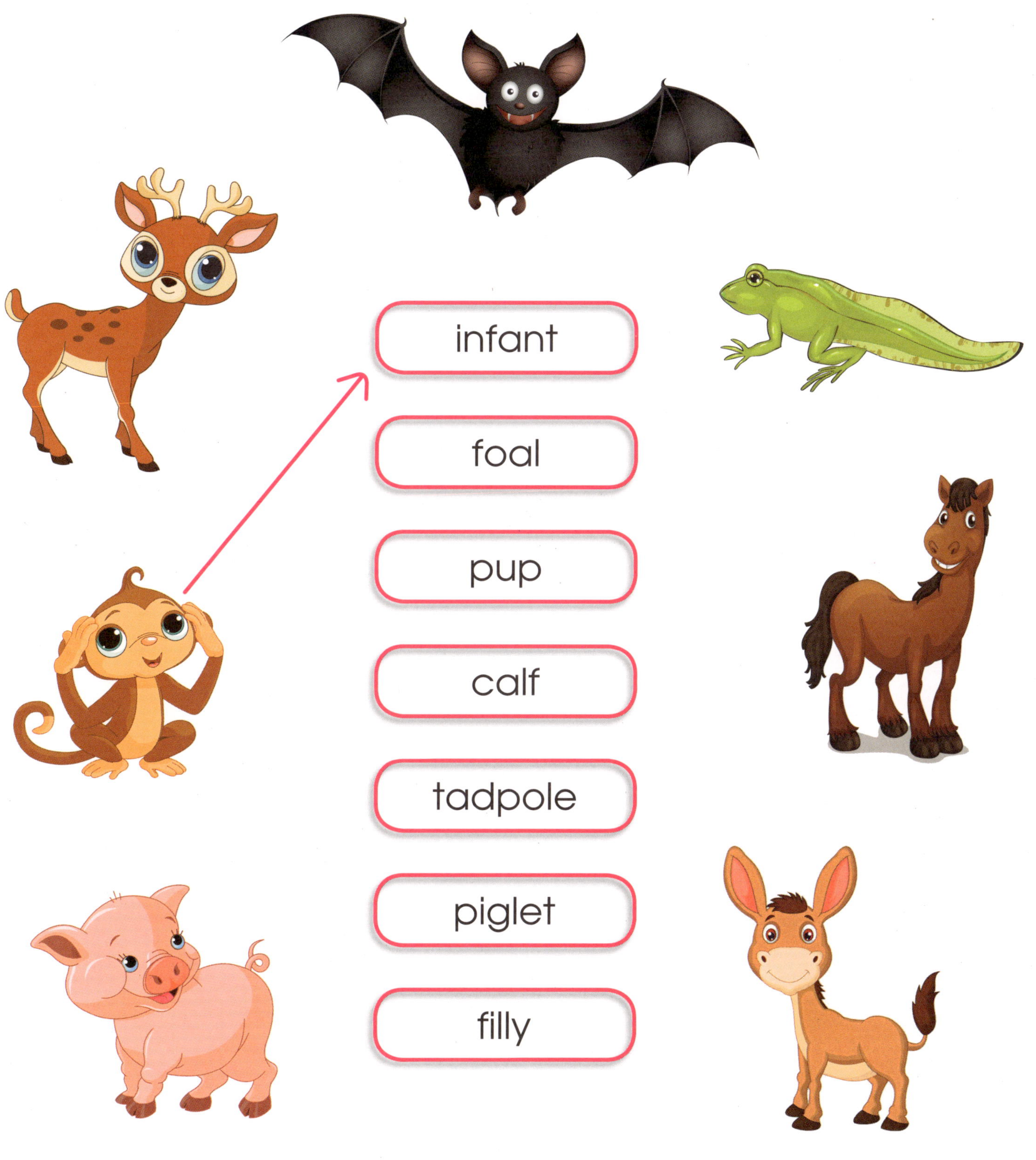

Partner Hunt

Spot and circle the opposite genders of the clue words in the grid below.

man	nephew	prince	monk
boy	bachelor	uncle	groom
	king	host	

f	x	v	n	s	h	j	x	a	t	h	j	i	k	o	l	o	h
k	w	t	u	i	w	h	k	v	c	p	f	a	u	k	y	a	g
j	q	v	n	o	m	j	k	t	e	p	o	d	f	c	l	i	w
h	l	t	l	s	i	l	h	n	p	r	q	p	i	e	d	s	s
k	f	d	q	f	l	a	d	x	a	i	w	o	m	a	n	o	k
h	u	k	m	z	b	w	q	n	p	n	b	q	u	e	e	n	p
o	z	t	m	k	c	j	j	c	z	c	r	m	n	i	e	c	e
s	z	j	m	t	c	j	r	e	a	e	i	b	o	d	o	w	b
t	u	t	d	a	u	n	t	g	x	s	d	f	t	w	b	h	f
e	o	o	k	v	l	e	a	i	d	s	e	g	q	s	m	x	t
s	a	w	a	d	p	r	e	r	h	q	c	u	g	d	u	h	m
s	n	x	g	h	x	u	z	l	s	p	i	n	s	t	e	r	p

HUMAN TERRITORY

Fill in the blanks with letters to complete the names of different houses. Then, match the pictures to the correct names.

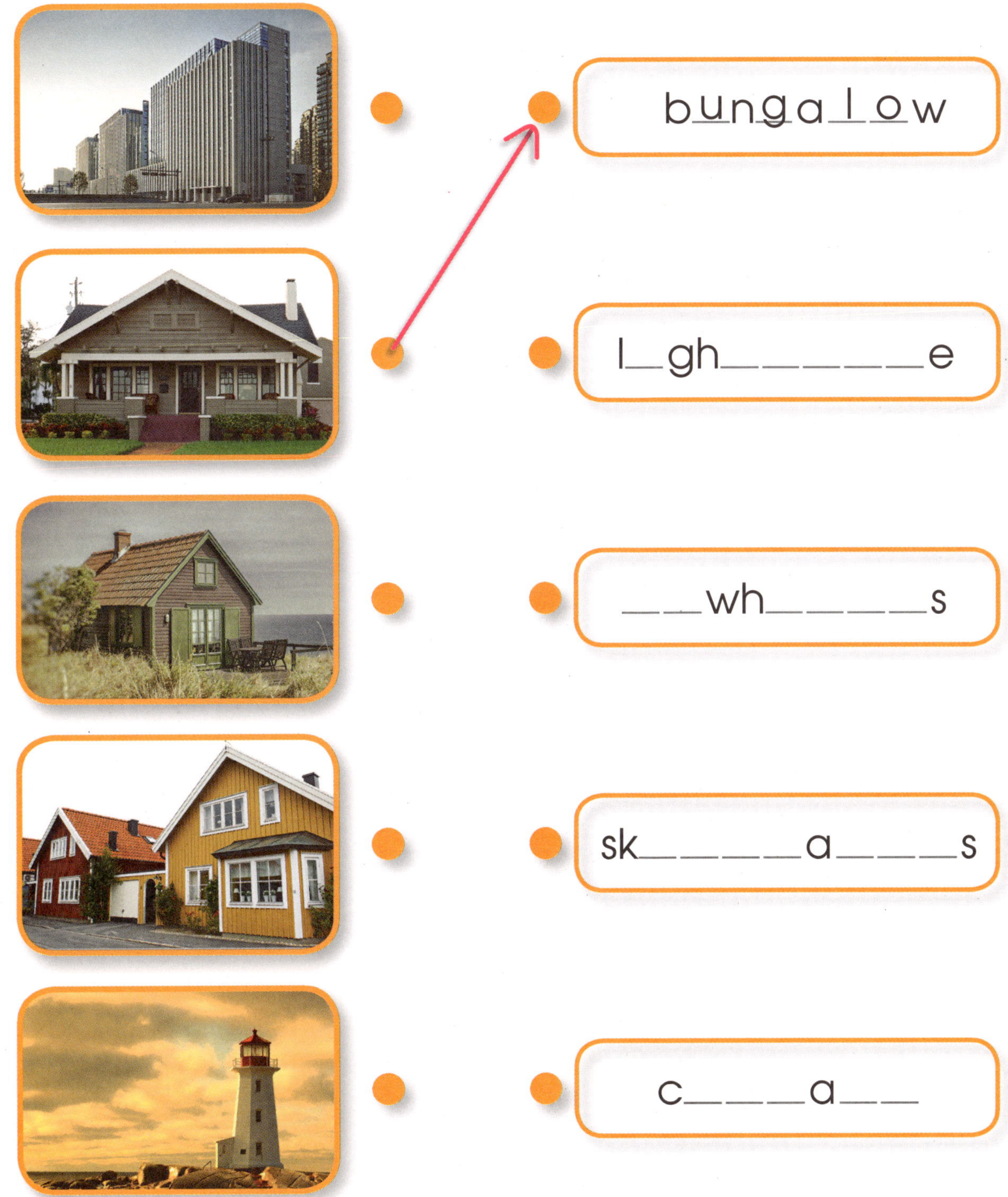

Treasure Hunt

Help the Vocabird reach the treasure chest by answering the clues in the treasure hunt.

Treasure Hunt

I make furniture.
I am a

________________.

I do magic tricks. I am a

________________.

I fly a plane.
I am a

________________.

I design houses.
I am an

________________.

Meaningful Match

Match the words to the correct baskets.

Voca tip: Use a dictionary to understand the correct meanings of the words.

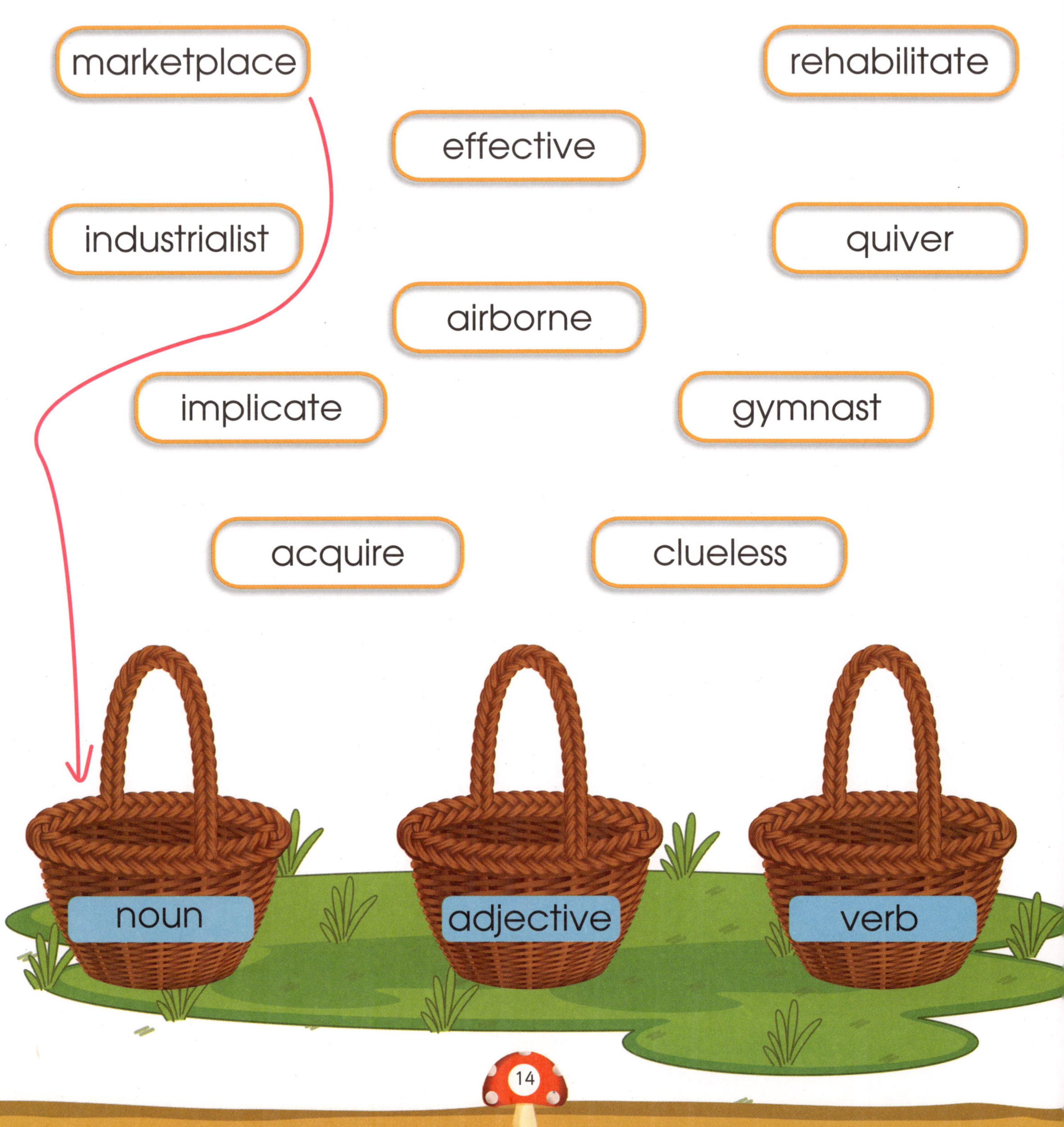

Wordy Woes

Write the meanings of the words below. Don't forget to use the dictionary!

1) vigil: ______________________________

2) unannounced:
____

3) glitz: ______________________________

4) clinic: ______________________________

5) farmer: ______________________________

6) hothouse: ______________________________

7) grocer: ______________________________

8) by-product: ______________________________

Sporty Words

Match the pictures to the sports they are used in.

WORDY JUMBLE

Look at the pictures and unscramble the letters to name them.

ntoorim

monitor
____

erte

____

tnriper

____

yoaekrdb

____

keojr

____

tbleaoopns

____

paple

____

Abstract Hunt

Help the Vocabird to fill in the blanks with suitable abstract nouns from the words below.

courage	fear	beauty
beliefs	bravery	education

1) The soldier was awarded a gold medal for his bravery.

2) She was known all over the village for her __________.

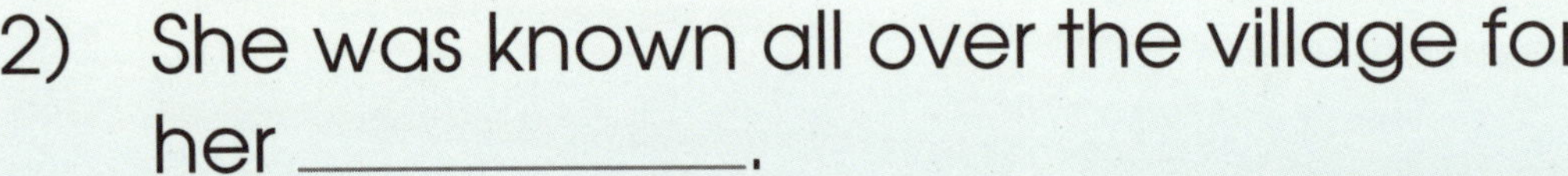

3) Nicole went into the haunted house because she felt no __________.

4) It took a lot of __________ for the little mouse to pull the lion's whiskers.

5) His religious __________ were very different from the rest of the town.

6) __________ is the most powerful weapon that you can use to change the world.

Word Builders

Change just one letter in each word to make a new word and help the Vocabird complete the word ladder.

AMAZING ANTONYMS

Fill in the blanks with the antonyms of the underlined words.

1) Ron was absent but Shaun was present for the test.

2) I was about to start writing the book, but the phone rang and I had to __________ the conversation first.

3) You should drink one glass of water in the morning as well as at __________.

4) Since that seat was occupied, I took the seat that was __________.

5) The weather was so cold that my aunt gave us __________ soup to drink.

6) You should meet with Uncle Sam as he wants to sell his car and you want to __________ one.

7) Except for one incorrect answer, all the other answers given by Peggy are __________.

Syno-List

Look at the words on the leaves and help the Vocabird write their synonyms on the next leaf.

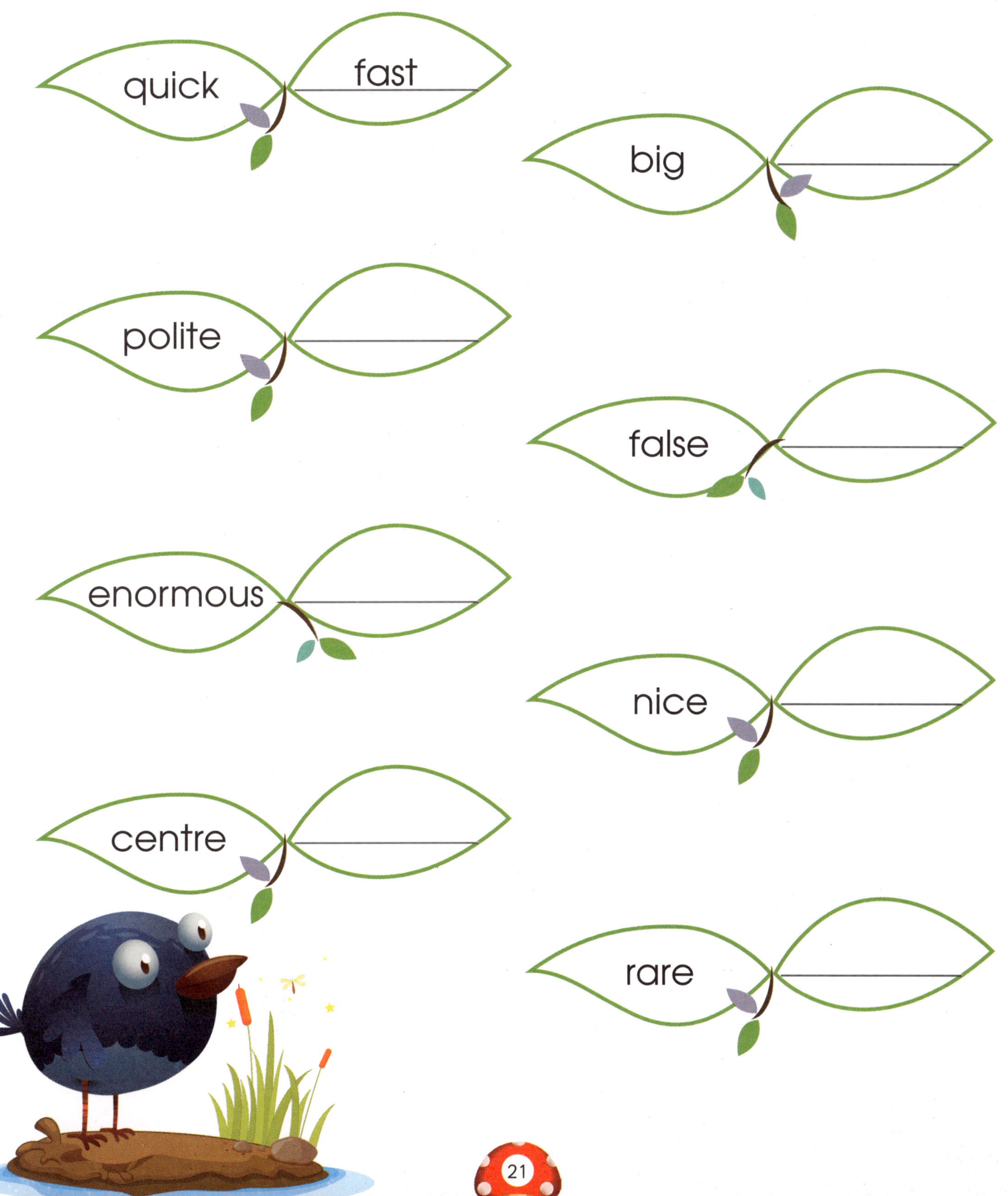

Compounding Words

Read the sentences and underline the compound words.

One day, I went to the playground with my friend.

We saw a rainbow.

It started to rain, so we wore our raincoats.

I felt a raindrop on my tongue.

The workers were doing some roadwork.

There was a roadblock.

We selected a different route.

I saw a sandbag that looked like sandpaper.

I also saw a sandstone.

I ate some delicious seafood.

I went on a boat and I got seasick.

I then saw a snowman.

He disappeared in the snowstorm.

Stringing Sentences

Help the Vocabird make new sentences with the words below.

playground - ______________________________

____

rainbow - ______________________________

____

raincoats - ______________________________

____

sandbag - ______________________________

____

seaweed - ______________________________

____

BAFFLING "B"

Write the meanings of the homonyms that begin with "b". Don't forget to refer to the dictionary.

Voca tip: Homonyms are words which have the same pronunciation but different meanings. In some cases, the spellings can be identical too.

bawled

bald

band

banned

bear

bare

birth

berth

Homograph Hunt

Read the meanings and fill in the blanks with the correct homograph from the words below.

Voca tip: Homographs are words which have the same spelling but different meanings and pronunciations.

compact	fine	row	wound
desert	proceeds	wind	frequent

MEANINGS	HOMOGRAPH
1) Small/to make small	compact
2) To abandon/a hot, arid region	______
3) Very good/delicate	______
4) Occurring regularly/to visit a place with regularity	______
5) A fight/to propel a boat forward using oars/a line	______
6) To turn/moving air	______
7) Turned/an injury	______
8) Advances/continues	______

Correcting Homophones

Some homophones are spelt incorrectly. Underline them and write the correct word on the blanks below.

Voca tip: Homophones are words which have the same pronunciation but different spellings and meanings.

Last knight, I was feeling a bit blew. I new I wood not do well in the test today but eye was surprised buy the easy questions. Who had made the paper? It seamed so easy. I was shore it had bean maid especially for me and I was caught up in delight when I read the questions. I wish all the exams were that easy forever, so that my piece will not be disturbed butt I knew nun of this would ever happen again.

night

Awesome Articles

Fill in the blanks with "a" or "an".

Voca tip: "A" is used before consonants and "an" is used before vowels.

It was __a__ starry night and Sam sat by his window, wishing for _____ pet. "I just want _____ animal, God. It could be _____ dog, _____ cat, _____ elephant, _____ hamster, _____ owl, _____ eagle, just about anything. But, I really want _____ pet. Please give me one!"

God looked down upon innocent Sam. He smiled and thought, "Maybe I should gift him _____ animal. But what could it be? Should I gift him _____ dog, _____ cat, _____ elephant or _____ owl? What if he is unable to take care of _____ pet? After all, looking after _____ pet is not _____ easy job. One has to feed it regularly, take good care of it and most importantly, give it lots of love."

Spell Check

Help the Vocabird correct the spellings of the words below.

Voca tip: Use a dictionary to check the spellings.

criticle critical

refaranse ________

margen ________

activity ________

fhysical ________

chauk ________

oppasite ________

Peppy Prepositions

Help the Vocabird tick the sentence with the correct preposition.

Voca tip: Prepositions are words which show the relationship between nouns or pronouns and other words in the sentence. For example: on, in, under, from, to, etc.

The cake is on the plate. ✓

The cake is at the plate.

The clock fell on the ground.

The clock fell in the ground.

The swing is in the park.

The swing is at the park.

The car is parked under the bridge.

The car is parked at the bridge.

CONFUSING KANGAROOS

Help the Vocabird identify the kangaroo words and underline the baby words in them.

Answers

Page 2

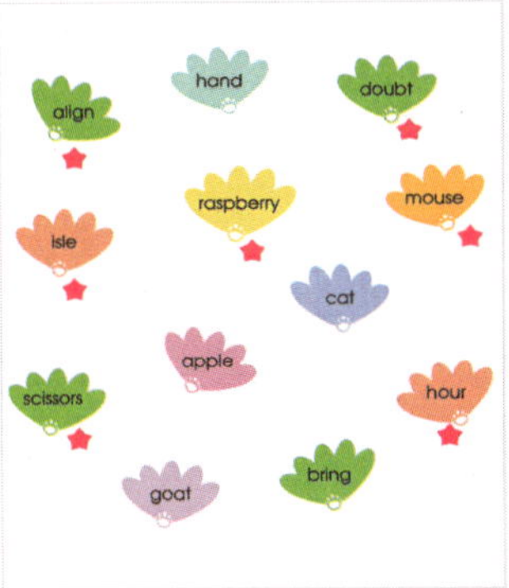

align
hand
doubt
raspberry
mouse
isle
cat
apple
scissors
hour
goat
bring

Page 3

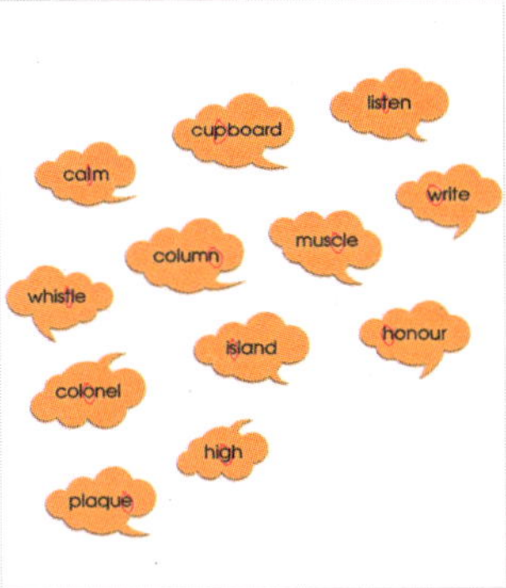

listen
cupboard
calm
write
column
muscle
whistle
island
honour
colonel
high
plaque

Page 4

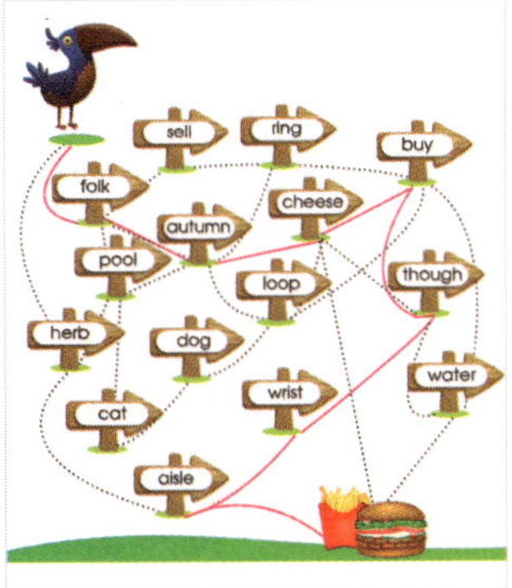

sell
ring
buy
folk
cheese
autumn
pool
though
loop
herb
dog
water
wrist
cat
aisle

Page 5

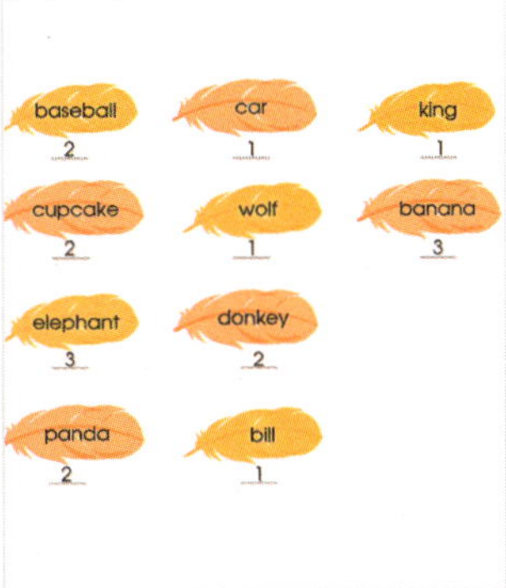

baseball
2
car
1
king
1
cupcake
2
wolf
1
banana
3
elephant
3
donkey
2
panda
2
bill
1

Page 6

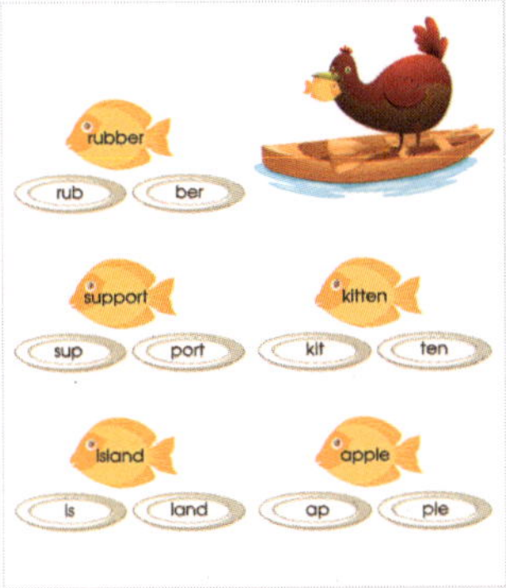

rubber
rub
ber
support
sup
port
kitten
kit
ten
island
is
land
apple
ap
ple

Page 7

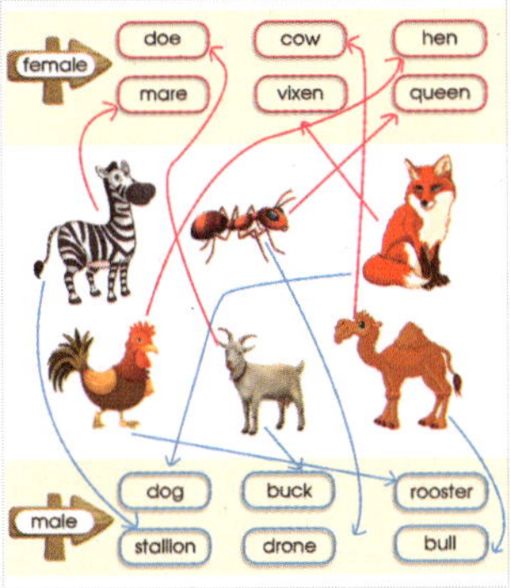

female
doe
cow
hen
mare
vixen
queen
male
dog
buck
rooster
stallion
drone
bull

Page 8

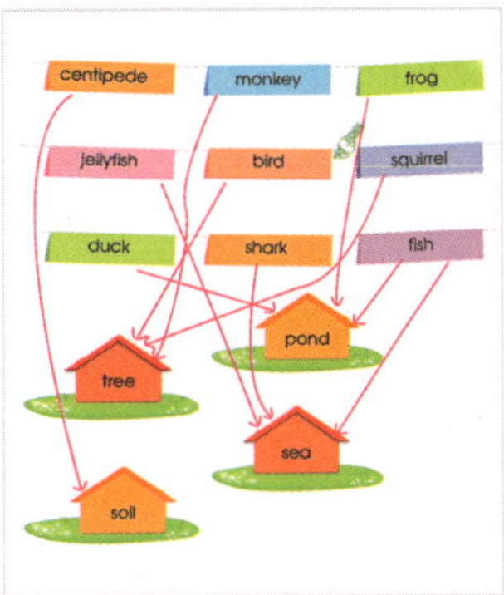

centipede
monkey
frog
jellyfish
bird
squirrel
duck
shark
fish
tree
pond
sea
soil

Page 9

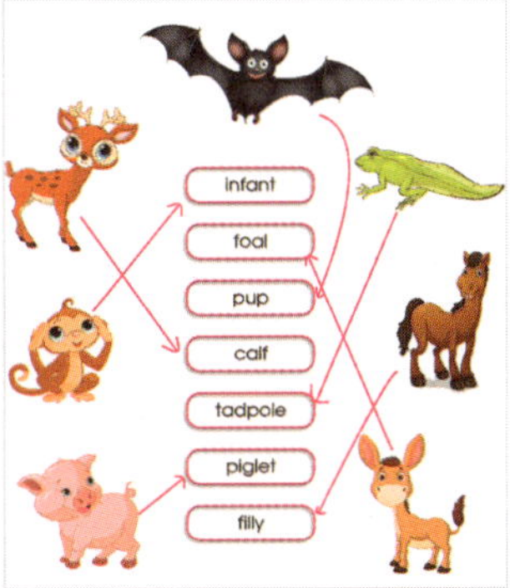

infant
foal
pup
calf
tadpole
piglet
filly

Page 10

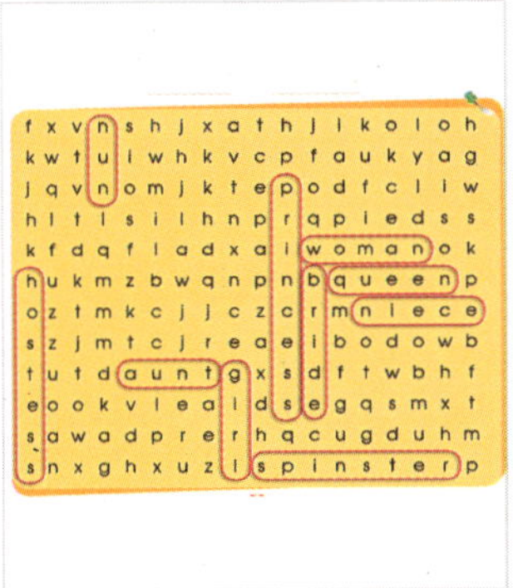

Page 11

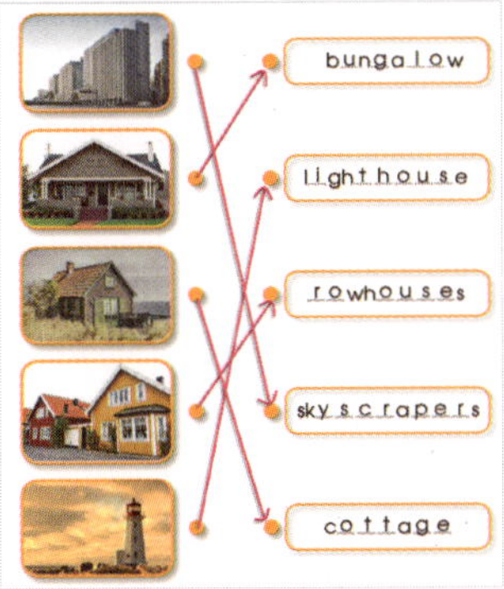

bungalow
lighthouse
rowhouses
skyscrapers
cottage

Page 12

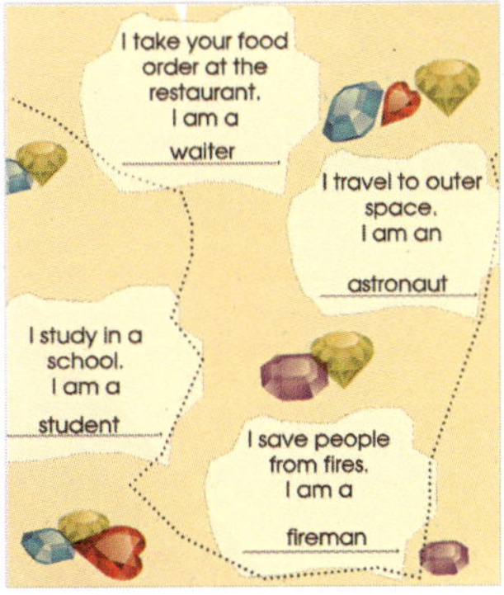

I take your food order at the restaurant. I am a
waiter
I travel to outer space. I am an
astronaut
I study in a school. I am a
student
I save people from fires. I am a
fireman

Page 13

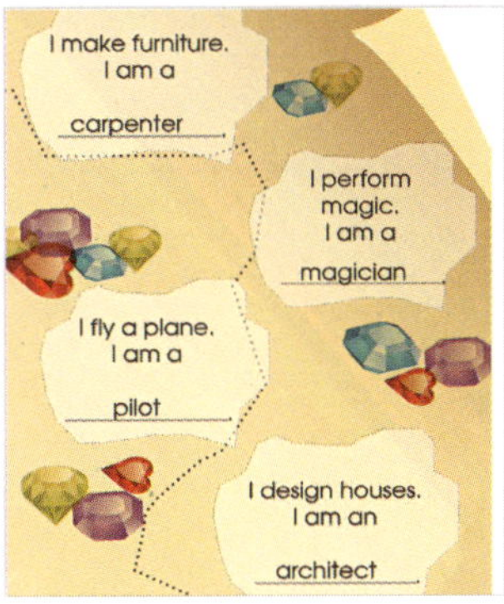

I make furniture. I am a
carpenter
I perform magic. I am a
magician
I fly a plane. I am a
pilot
I design houses. I am an
architect

Page 14

marketplace
rehabilitate
effective
industrialist
quiver
airborne
implicate
gymnast
acquire
clueless
noun
adjective
verb

Page 15

ANSWERS WILL VARY

Page 16

hockey
football
table tennis
basketball
badminton

Page 17

ntoorim
monitor
erte
tree
tnriper
printer
yoaekrdb
keyboard
keojr
joker
tbleaoopns
tablespoon
paple
apple

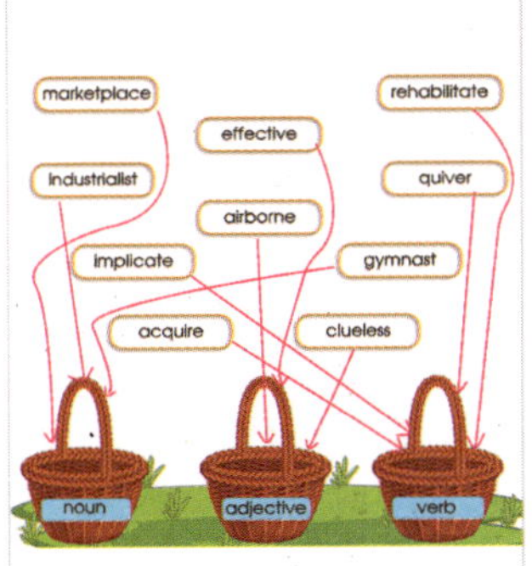

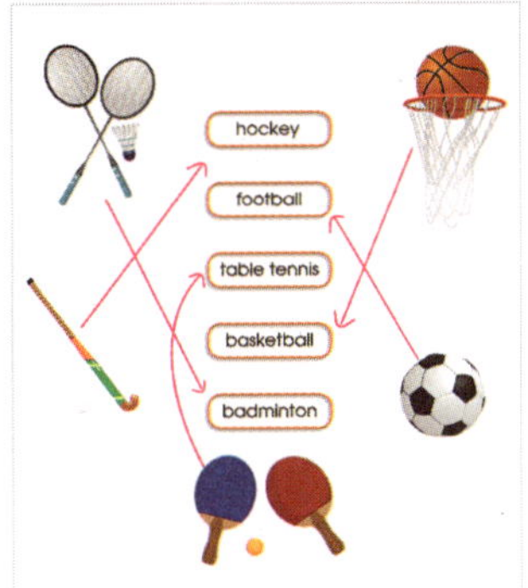

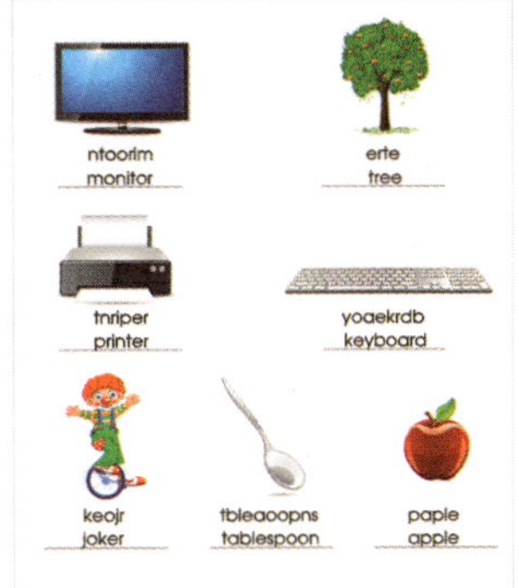

Answers

Page 18

1) The soldier was awarded a gold medal for his bravery.
2) She was known all over the village for her beauty.
3) Nicole went into the haunted house because she felt no fear.
4) It took a lot of courage for the little mouse to pull the lion's whiskers.
5) His religious beliefs were very different from the rest of the town.
6) Education is the most powerful weapon that you can use to change the world.

Page 19

ANSWERS WILL VARY

Page 20

1) Ron was absent but Shaun was present for the test.
2) I was about to start writing the book,but the phone rang and I had to finish the conversation first.
3) You should drink one glass of water in the morning as well as at night.
4) Since that seat was occupied, I took the seat that was unoccupied.
5) The weather was so cold that my aunt gave us hot soup to drink.
6) You should meet with Uncle Sam as he wants to sell his car and you want to buy one.
7) Except for one incorrect answer, all the other answers given by Peggy are correct.

Page 21

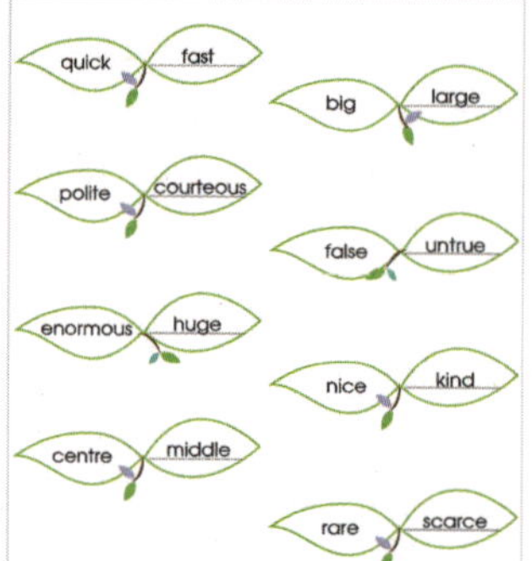

Page 22

One day, I went to the playground with my friend.
We saw a rainbow.
It started to rain, so we wore our raincoats.
I felt a raindrop on my tongue.
The workers were doing some roadwork.
There was a roadblock.
We selected a different route.
I saw a sandbag that looked like sandpaper.
I also saw a sandstone.
I ate some delicious seafood.
I went on a boat and I got seasick.
I then saw a snowman.
He disappeared in the snowstorm.

Page 23

ANSWERS WILL VARY

Page 24

ANSWERS WILL VARY

Page 25

MEANINGS	HOMOGRAPH
1) Small/to make small	compact
2) To abandon/a hot, arid region	desert
3) Very good/delicate	fine
4) Occurring regularly/to visit a place with regularity	frequent
5) A fight/to propel a boat forward using oars/a line	row
6) To turn/moving air	wind
7) Turned/an injury	wound
8) Advances/continues	proceeds

Page 26

Last knight, I was feeling a bit blew. I new I wood not do well in the test today but eye was surprised buy the easy questions. Who had made the paper? It seamed so easy? I was shore it had bean maid especially for me and I was caught up in delight when I read the questions. I wish all the exams were that easy forever, so that my piece will not be disturbed butt I knew nun of this would ever happen again.

night	I	made
blue	by	peace
knew	seemed	but
would	sure	none
	been	

Page 27

It was a starry night and Sam sat by his window, wishing for a pet. "I just want an animal, God. It could be a dog, a cat, an elephant, a hamster, an owl, an eagle, just about anything. But, I really want a pet. Please give me one!"

God looked down upon innocent Sam. He smiled and thought, "Maybe I should gift him an animal. But what could it be? Should I gift him a dog, a cat, an elephant or an owl? What if he is unable to take care of a pet? After all, looking after a pet is not an easy job. One has to feed it regularly, take good care of it and most importantly, give it lots of love."

Page 28

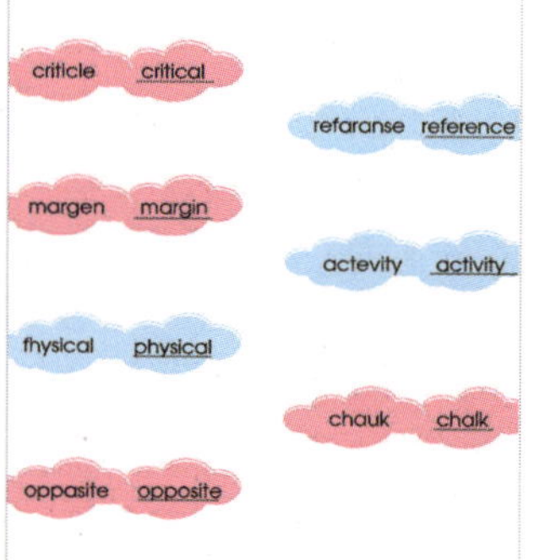

Page 29

Page 30